FIVE WOMEN

WINNER OF THE

Willow Run Poetry Book Award

Hidden River Arts offers the Willow Run Poetry Book Award for an unpublished collection of poetry, in English, of 75 to 100 pages. The award provides $1000 and publication by Hidden River Publishing on its Hidden River Press imprint.

Hidden River Arts is an interdisciplinary arts organization dedicated to supporting and celebrating the unserved artists among us, particularly those outside the artistic and academic mainstream.

FIVE WOMEN

ROSETTA MARANTZ COHEN

HIDDEN RIVER PRESS

Philadelphia   2024

Cover image by Damianius
Design and typography by P. M. Gordon Associates, Inc.
Library of Congress Control Number: 2024948573
ISBN 979-8-9854317-9-7

HIDDEN RIVER PRESS
An imprint of Hidden River Publishing
Philadelphia, Pennsylvania

Contents

Acknowledgments

Word Problems, *Feminist Quarterly*. Volume 46, Number 1, 2005.

There were six of us at dinner: *Feminist Quarterly*. Volume 46, Number 1, 2020.

The Famous Poet, The Kiss, Children and Facts: In *The Town of Insomniacs* (chapbook: Finishing Line Press, December, 2018).

Spartan Woman: *Arkana*, Issue 11, December, 2021.

Land Grant School, Gifts from Foreigners: *The Road Not Taken*, Spring, 2023.

Four Women

Spartan Woman

I sing the light of Agido: I see her like the sun, which Agito is now calling as a witness. But the renowned leader does not let me praise or blame her.

Alcman, 7th C BCE (*Poetarum Melicorum Graecorum Fragmenta*)

1. Bride

We had chosen each other, as is customary,
by groping blindly in a dark room
filled with other men and other women.
My mother helped me plot my strategy:
feeling for height first, then the width
of the chest, then sufficient hair
for potency. When my husband's
wild hands first found my breasts, I was sure
the gods had blessed us.

First, they shaved my head, smooth as a stone,
then exchanged my woman's chiton
for a man's, a crimson *chlamys* draped
on my narrow shoulders;
even Laconian boots were given
to me, whose soles were unaccustomed
to the feel of hide,
having lived unshod for eighteen years,
winter and summer.

It was spring. Others had come
before us; women I had known
since childhood playing in the yellow fields,
studying together. Others, like ourselves,
moved in somber pairs
down the long arcade, flanked by priests.
Crows reeled overhead.
A warm winter
promised a lucky spring.

Past the old men and the wives
who had taught me letters, past

                                          Rosetta Marantz Cohen

the sun-dried, mud-brick
houses of my town,
wended the long processional,
the cattle mantled in flowers, music
from lutes; a skin
drum beating like a heart,
entering first our ears and then our bodies.

Teiresias claims that a woman's
capacity for sexual pleasure
is nine times greater than a man's. I suspect
that my husband derives
little pleasure from my body, cares
little when I am given to his brother,
nor is his pleasure greater
with other women; one
woman's body being the same as another's.

Nights, when he steals forth from his barracks,
crossing with stealth the black fields to our dark home,
entering me, as the gods ordain,
my face hidden, my body
given over for its purpose,
I sense his duty and distaste.
Done, he returns to his bed among men.
I ask the gods for a child, but
they do not hear me, or perhaps
hearing me, do not wish to respond.

By summer, my hair returns, a dark
helmet, like a helot's cap.
I am exiled from the naked
play of my sisters. No one
admires my body in the day,

and at night, I cannot remember
with whom I have slept, so many men come and leave
in the dark. And still there is no sign
of a coming child.

I miss the days of my youth,
my time among girls and women,
speech that elicited speech.
When the polis took notice
of me, it was then that
my life ended.

2. Mother

First I submerged her in wine,
as the elders commanded;
and small though she was
she survived that bitter trial
hardly noticing, it seemed,
the acrid bite and stain
on her near-transparent skin.

I held her little back erect,
her feet pressed up
against the bucket's edge
as the priests declared her worthy
of her life. Here,
said the elders,
she will live among us,
female though she is,
with a plot of land—a yellow field, her dowry
and her stake—passed,
should the gods decree it,
to many sons.

Some are stillborn,
making of the womb
a compassionate grave.
Others die after birth,
their deaths decreed by the elders—
being too small, too weak, too cleft
of lip, too lame,
or cursed by the gods:
unwhole in mind;

some for the crime of being
not a male—destined merely
to breed and not to kill.
All pass violently from life
on the cliff of Apothetae,
having wasted the state
nine useless months in the womb,
which, emptied now, is free
to be filled again.

Rosetta Marantz Cohen

3. Confession

The elders herald above all else
the birth of a son;

call the woman who bears sons
among the blessed: Sisters of Hera,

most precious of Spartans,
praised by the poets. Sons

who are turned into strangers
to those who bore them,

taken and turned in their seventh year
by brutal men to brutal ways,

schooled in the edicts of cunning;
vicious, venal, lovers of blood,

competing for the honor of most
cruel; courting hunger and thirst

as if deprivation were itself a god.
Who would want this son? I am asking you,

secret, precious, invisible Self,

knowing that you alone
will understand my question.

4. Daughter

Having no sons beyond their seventh year,
my father made me his son, his beloved,
his constant companion.
Then came word that my brothers
had died with great honor in war
and there followed, of course, rejoicing,

since dying with honor in battle
turned men into demigods.
The poets sang of their exploits,
sang of the gold thrones
on which they now sat,
feasting with the immortals.

My mother tied red cloth to the door frames,
burned incense for the gods, and danced
for joy in the public square.
Each morning gifts would be placed
at our gate: wine, sweets, a linen
cloth stitched with their names—

those blessed and most precious dead.
I remained here. A mere
body with breasts and a womb,
but brave, strong, ready
to shoulder the work
of adult life.

My father would come
and sit with me at the table,
talk about politics, the demands
of the gods which always seemed
so burdensome to me.

Rosetta Marantz Cohen

He spoke to me like a friend, asked
Should he plow now or later?

asked how he might settle
a dispute with a selfish neighbor.
I was wise in the way that women are,
and gave him counsel. *Father
and daughter*, he said, as if
the sound of that phrase gave pleasure:

You, he said, *my patroiokos,
shall inherit my fields and my cattle.*
When he died,
a part of me was laid too
in his narrow grave.

5. Memory

My body was most my own
when I ran
through the streets of Elis
during the races of Heraea.
We who were virgins,
whose bodies were strongest and most nimble,
ran the same course as men,
steep and circuitous;
our hair falling
about our backs and arms,
our arms sun-brown
from the long practices that prepared us.

At the starting signal gong
we lept like Cerynitian hinds,
free in the open air,
unfettered by age or marriage,
in the heat of the day,
in the name of Hera,
for a crown of olives,
raced through the dust
that stained our legs,
and painted ochre
our dark hair.

At dusk, we came
together as friends;
winners and losers,
our bodies
filled with the good ache of use,
gathering to feast
in the open air, the sky

Rosetta Marantz Cohen

darkening, the cool
evening salving our limbs.
We told each other:
If we died today
we would count ourselves
among the blessed.

6. Old Age

In youth, we are all different;
some lovely, some plain,
fertile or barren; some
rich with family and friends
crowding their tables; others
solitary, silent, stooped in service
to those they neither love nor hate.

In age, we are the same; coming
together as sisters before death;
stripped of any gifts that distinguished
one from another. Even wealth—
the fine foods or luxurious beds
that made one proud and another
covetous—fall away as appetite
falls away; as sight falters
and one bed or rug is finally
like another.

Now, the memories of pleasure
contract like the memories of pain
into a single darkness;
until as one we move together
into a common sleep,
hoping at last
that the gods are real,
but sharing, towards death,
a deepening sense
they are not.

Anchoress

*I long to see her bodily presence while I am here,
her blessed soul: her truth, her wisdom, her
charity; whereby I may learn to know myself
and reverently dread my God. And when our
good Lord said: Wilt thou see her? I answered
and said: Yea, good Lord, I thank Thee; yea,
good Lord, if it be Thy will. Oftentimes I
prayed this, and I weened to have seen her
in bodily presence, but I saw her not so.*

Juliana of Norwich
(*Revelations of Divine Love*, 1373)

1. Daybreak

Beside me, morning clover;
a trinity of green
distinguishing itself from grass
as saints from common men.
Three eyes it casts upon me;
a face-to-face; a stare,
Not pointing to another world
but praising what is here.

Rosetta Marantz Cohen

2. Revelation

What should have brought me
closer to heaven, has brought
me closer to earth;
its musky, excremental
particularity
that assumes
through intimacy
an increasing radiance.

What should have brought me
closer to god,
has brought only astonishment
of the body,
daily revelations that were
before invisible: its divinations,
its prayerful complaints
that start out not in the heart
but in the materiality
of the bruised limb, the
insistent bladder, the sudden release—
like Christ's love made real—
of a cramp or throb.

Miracle is the very ground
that without summons of prayer
will move from dampness into heat;
or the sun that angles forth
from my tiny window,
its penetrating light
a ritual, that catachyzes
hour after hour
this blessed lack.

3. A Month of Prayers

Matins	Matins	Matins	Matins	Matins	Matins
Lauds	Lauds	Lauds	Lauds	Lauds	Lauds
Prime	Prime	Prime	Prime	Prime	Prime
Terce	Terce	Terce	Terce	Terce	Terce
Sext	Sext	Sext	Sext	Sext	Sext
None	None	None	None	None	None
Vespers	Vespers	Vespers	Vespers	Vespers	Vespers
Compline	Compline	Compline	Compline	Compline	Compline

Matins	Matins	Matins	Matins	Matins	Matins
Lauds	Laud	Lauds	Lauds	Laud	Lauds
Prime	Prime	Prime	Prime	Prmie	Prime
Terce	Terce	Terce	Terce	Terce	Terce
Sext	Sext	Sxet	Sext	Sext	Texts
None	None	None	Noen	None	None
Vespers	Vespers	Vespers	Vespers	Vespers	Vespers
Compline	Colpine	Compline	Complne	Compline	Compline

Matin	Matin	Matin	Matin	Matin	Matin
Lauds	Laud	Lauds	Laud	Lauds	Lauds
Prime	Prime	Prime	Prime	Prmie	Primwe
Terce	Terce	Terse	Terce	Terce	terse
Sext	Sext	Sxet	Sext	Sext	
None	None	None	Noen	None	Nonw
Vespers	Vespers	Vespers	Vespers	vespers	Vespers
Compline	Complice	Compline	Compline	Compline	Complice

Matins	Matins	Matins	Matins	Matins	Matins
Lauds	Lduas	lauds	laud	Lauds	Audls
Prime	prime	Pirme	Prime	Pmrie	Prime
Terce	terce	Trece	Terce	Tcree	terce
Sext	Sext	Sext	Sext	sext	Sext
None	None	None	Nones	None	Nnone
Vespers	Vesters	Vespers	vesper	Vsper	Vspres
Compline	Compline	Compline		compline	compline

Matins	Matins	Matins	Matins	matins	snitam
Lauds	Lauds	Lauds	LUSds	:auds	lauds
Prime	Prime	Prime	Prime	prime	Prime
Terce	Terce	terce	Terce	Terce	Terce
Sext	Sexts	sext	sext	sex	tSext
None	None	None	None	None	None
Vespers	Vespers	vespers	spvers	sverps	vespers
Complice	compine	compline	Compline	Compline	Ecilpmoc

4. Confession 1

A leper came to my squint
to beg for bread and prayer.
I had no bread I said
and as for prayer,
I prayed that he
would leave me
to my own despair.

I beg forgiveness now
for what I thought and said.
I had no prayers for him
but I'd had bread.

5. Sin

Riven by distance and air, still
I cling to the priest's
shuffle, the rumble
of argument. Sound
drifts like blown
snow settling
onto the limbs
of birches.

All that ties me to the world,
all that anchors this body
to earth, seeps incessantly
in, and the body
cleaves to it
despite every form
of renunciation.

The Book of Rules
says, *Bride of God, throw off*
the gown of the world,
the mantle of senses.
Come to Christ newborn,
lulled by the music of heaven.

And still, the miller's
wretched cough,
the caw of the crow,
the cruel scrape of the plow
on frigid soil
enters me like a lover,
eager and faithless.

6. Confession 2

Open your heart, says the Lord,
no penance is beyond absolution.

Rapists, thieves, men
who have ruined beauty,

to me, God's bride, come. All
who destroy and ravage,

bring their sour, disembodied,
breath to the squint. Their false

penance; their repulsive pride
enshrouded in terror. *Please,*

they whisper, *pray for my sins*
that took, for my own pleasure,

innocence; degraded, consumed,
corrupted, impoverished, slandered.

Into the darkness of this sacred
space; the harrowing silence

of this enclosure, I am charged
with forgiveness, a charge

more difficult to endure than any deprivation;
since the heart, itself enclosed in its secret space,

is even more silent, dark and impenetrable.

                                                    Rosetta Marantz Cohen

The Accuser

What God do witches pray to?

Salem magistrates (Salem town
records; February 4, 1692)

1. October

With the chill
wind off Will's Hill
chanting *fall, fall,*
fall is coming,
Jane and I towards
Salem Neck walked
into the bright morning,
past the ashen stalks
of spent corn,
past the chestnut
tree tithing its seeds
into the palm
of the street.
There was a maple
grasping its last
blood-red leaves;
others, like
hymnal pages,
darkening underfoot.
Glory to God,
we said, *who*
makes this temporal
beauty for our sake.
Who makes for us
Beauty and death,
Beauty in death
that we might understand.

2. January

Morning, church, a strangeness.
Shadows play on the floor like pressed keys
moving across a soundless instrument.
Someone's cough becomes the bark of a bear.
Crow on the rimed ledge of the parsonage
casts the shadow of a gloved hand.
Then a gust at the sanctuary door,
throwing open the latch . . .
"Believe in the Lord and He
shall make thee whole." The Reverend
Parris raises his fists to the sky:
"Fire shall rain down, verily," he says,
"for even the sin of sinful thought."

By afternoon, the snow home-strands us here,
crouched by the smoldering hearth. My sister Jane
and I play idly at what games we can.
Our naming game labels the shapes in the fire:
She sees two hands in prayer, a pair of trees;
I see the face of a woman, licked by flame.

Before the early dark enshrouds the barn,
Mother (angry always, always at nothing)
sends me out for kindling, anything
blown down from the bare trees.
A meerkat, bone thin, eyes my every move.
Something fleeting scuttles by the house.
Everything seems dead or soon to die,
and the wind sings *Soon, Soon* like an elegy
over the gutted garden and the yard.

Evening, we sit by the last heat of the hearth.
Father fulminates on the new tax
levied against our farm, and mother
pricks herself as she mends. Her quiet curse
rises like a cloud in the cold air.

3. March

Haunted, the winter fields beyond the house.
On bitter nights, stilled by the stubborn cold,
we hear them call to us, the living dead,
finding their way beneath the drafty pane.
In terrible voices, we can hear them speak,
luring us out of faith and into sin.

Christ the Redeemer shelters us from sin.
Still, some strangeness lives within the house:
voices that seem to whisper as we speak
our prayers, or pass around us as a cold
chill. Jane, standing by the window pane,
said that she saw the face of our long-dead

neighbor, Goody Parsons, rise from the dead,
goading her, through fiery threats, to sin
against our Lord. Jane broke the glass pane,
Father had newly purchased for the house.
Now, even by the hearth, it is always cold,
and nothing can stop the voices when they speak.

And now it seems unceasingly they speak:
Who can distinguish the Living from the Dead?
Who can distinguish the Fire from the Cold?
Who can distinguish Righteousness from Sin?
Their questions fly like bats about the house
and write themselves in rime on the broken pane.

Yesterday, my sister writhed with pain,
her body wracked and contorted. When she spoke,
it was in a strange voice, and the house
seemed to reverberate with the souls of the dead.

Reverend Parris prayed with us. Sin,
he said, would consume us all, his voice cold

as the frozen fields, a cold
that has entered me now. Pain
seers my body. Tempted to sin,
tempted to speak
evil by the dead
I rail in agony about the house.

Cold, Sin,
House, Pain—
The dead speak our names.

                                        Rosetta Marantz Cohen

4. May

Ylhe helss leho esso
Nohoyd siemma elstour ree
Slenc foom soleeta hool
Lattf oer tool loccat pree.

5. June

On the body of Christ, I testify
that Miss Sarah Good appeared to me
in spectral form on the 8 of May.

What did this specter do or say?

She appeared at my bedside: Sarah Good,
dressed as she stands here dressed today,
demanding I curse the Living God.
A specter of fire, she tore at me,
wielding a knife blade, licked by flame,
she ravaged my bedclothes, grabbed my throat.
See on my neck where the bruises remain?
See on my arms the shape of her hands?
In a sulfurous cloud she flew at me
barking her cruel, satanic demands—
she moved without ever touching the ground.
When I tried to cry out, I could make no sound.

Are you certain the vision was Sarah Good?

As certain as you are standing here.
As certain that all these men who judge
the truth of my words are sitting there.
The calico dress she wore is the same
as the calico dress she wears today.

How did you manage to flee her wrath?

We wrestled for hours. Life against Death.
My pillow and blanket were torn to shreds.
Mother can vouch for the truth of my words.
I fought with the strength of a hundred men.
Faith is my army, now as then.

     Rosetta Marantz Cohen

I summoned the angels and angels heard.
At last, the demon tired and fled.
What terrible strength you have, she'd said.

Thus, by your faith, she was defeated?

Thus, by my strength she was defeated,
now living to testify before man
and God what I saw and what I did.

So you swear to the truth of the things you have said?

In the name of Christ and the blessed dead,
I swear on my soul to the things I have said.

6. September

OnthesoulsofBridgetBishopMaria
MatherMarthaCarrierMarthaCorey
MaryEstySarahGoodElizabethHowSuzannah
MartinElizabethRebeccaDicerMargaret
NurseAlicePrinceMaryParkerMaryLacy
HannahCarrollProctorSarahWilson
AnnColeAnnPudeatorDeliveranceWilmot
AbigailHobbsMary ScottMaryWarren
JoanPenneyElizabethPaineMaryBlack
SarahBuckleyMary MarstonSarahRoots
AnnSearsElizabethFostickSarahWildes
SarahPeaseElizabethJohnsonDorcasGood
BeforeJesusourLordIrepentIrepentIrepent.

Pioneer Teacher

*In my school, I am content and happy for I
am doing good, but I am entirely deprived
of sympathy and good society. I have no
human being here in whom I can confide,
or who possesses kindred feelings with mine.
But there is One to whom I can go.*

From the letters of Ellen Lee,
Hamilton County Indiana, 1852

1. Story

One month after the death of my mother,
my father married a stranger
and brought her back to New Bedford
to fill up my mother's silence.
This was the way of things.
And though she was cruel and covetous
like witches in fairy tales,
I endured for the sake of my sisters
this woman's barked commands
and humiliations; the beautiful
rituals gone, replaced by vulgarity
and indifference. Through four
long winters without once
hearing spoken the name of my mother,
I endured, seeing this as a test
of my faith; since hardship,
they say, is a blessing
for those with the power of faith.

But when, in the dark hallway,
she stacked mother's books for burning,
and her dresses were shredded for rags,
and the last of her handiwork sold,
I resolved to escape. A single
woman, educated at home,
pious, penniless, wholly averse
to marriage—seeing the servitude
of that state, and the fleeting
nature of human loyalty—
I resolved to devote my life
to the poor and the weak, to those

                    Rosetta Marantz Cohen

not yet blessed with the power
of reading and writing.

Christ had said to endure. Christ
then said to escape. I heeded His call,
packed up my modest belongings
And resolved to become a teacher:
I had read about armies of women
using their lives like water
to meet the great thirst of the West.
A kind of secular saint-work,
a kind of monastic immersion.

Around me, in Hartford, women
much like myself assembled,
all clever, abandoned, devoted
to doing good. As one,
through the rigors of deep study,
we prepared ourselves for rebirth
in a strange and brutal place—
primitive, wild, a fallen
Eden, where men run lawless
and faithless, ignorant
of God. *Go! Go!*
said our teachers, *spread the balm
of belief by passing among them the balm
of reading, writing, and figuring.
Make of yourself an instrument of the Lord.
There, where the line between men
and beasts is hardly drawn, draw—
through books—a hard and persuasive line.
Make of yourself a model and a sign.*

For two long years I have studied
among women, taught by women,
befriended by women. Soon,
we will all be scattered;
sent, alone, to places,
near-womanless, remote.
An army of one, I will march
under the banner of God.

For my mother,
and in her name,
I commit myself to the task.

                                             Rosetta Marantz Cohen

2. Journey

First by train, then carriage
to Buffalo. By boat
from Buffalo on Lake Erie,

storm-tossed, sea-sick,
home-sick—on a berth
fit for a child—finally, to Cleveland

then to Sandusky; then by coach
to Cincinnati and another boat
to St. Louis where we'd wait

two days for a cargo of babies;
then on to Jefferson by stage,
then switched in DePauw

to a lumber wagon hauling
dung. Then, arriving two miles
short of the town line, on foot.

I am here. I am here.
A flat, treeless husk of a town:
courthouse, grocery, blacksmith,

grime baked in by sweltering heat,
and a veil of clay-dust over everything,
blown by a sour, nagging wind.

School is a dirt-floor box;
not desk nor chair to be found
anywhere, nor books nor pens,
nor writing implements. A pale light

drifts through the glassless window;
the damp hearth throws out chill,
and field mice scuttle above in the roof.

Here you be, says the mayor
under his long mustache. *Your
own domain readied for learning.*

Monday, five boys and a girl
stand at the open door.
One held a "book,"

an ancient postal register;
another, a catalogue
for feed and horse supplies.

None has seen a bath in weeks, or ever
a Bible from the way they talk: all
weren'ts and *ain'ts*

and taking His name in vain.
The one girl touched my skirt
like a cat would, rubbing her head

on my lap, and the boys
stood open-mouthed
at the sight of one so clean.

Much to do. The time passes.
It is hard to believe the weeks
that have passed since coming

and the sense of purpose that blossoms
like a bud, as the want of friendship
drifts out of my heart.

Much to do. Tomorrow, we'll look at the letters
F through H, and speak about soap,
and speak about God's grace.

3. Incident

According to the locals, it began
when a notorious drunk, a Mr. Smith,
questioned the virtue of the drunken wife
of another local drunk: one Bob McCann.
McCann, well-armed, appeared the following day
near Mercer's grocer, drunk of course, and set
to make this Smith apologize, or get
his "full and just" revenge some other way.
Curses, ungodly threats, and then a gun
pulled from its holster. Someone shouts, "Look out!"
and there's McCann, now turning to the shout
and drawing too, and firing. It was when
my mother died I last beheld a corpse;
today, I helped to lay out two of them,
and prayed for the wasted souls of wasted men,
closing their eyes, and sewing shut their lips;
and thinking of the work still to be done
and how, in this, I am the chosen one.

4. Eight Months

Eight months on the calendar. Eight months!
The days pass in a blur of work. Twenty
pupils now, and a Sunday school
filled with a wholly godless mass
of illiterate farmers, thieves, and hangers-on,
an Indian girl, a prospector enroute
to Santa Fe . . . all leaving a film of soot,
sweat, spit and dust on the makeshift pews.
Three young men, come lately from the east,
built desks for the school. The youngest one
proposed marriage after a single day. He said
I was the angel he had sought in the West.
But I am happy unwedded like never
before. Happy in my usefulness. A boy
of five or six (no one seems to know) asked
to live with me, his father being drunk
and brutal, and his mother dead. Months, he
lingered after school, like a stray cat, arranging
the slates or simply sitting silent. The child
had no name he knew; was just called "boy,"
he said, and then one day, I saw a ring of bruises
up his arms, and when I asked about them,
He pulled his sleeves down out of shame. I prayed
on what to do for a full week,
and then said yes that he could stay with me,
as a trial first. That was weeks ago. Now,
it is hard to imagine the lack of him in my little home.
Rough though he is, the boy—I named him Paul—
soaks up kindness like a parched plant! Feeding
him, talking every night, his scrubbed cheek
on its first pillow, resting; what more

could I ever ask for? When he comes
to the fire evenings with a book in his hand
and asks me to "tell a tale," my heart leaps.
When he smiles, truly I see God's grace
made manifest, clearer than any scripture,
and in my once-starved heart (though not yet
plainly to his face), I call him "son."

Rosetta Marantz Cohen

5. Family

Soon after she arrived—a small, serious
person, humbly dressed, schooled in Nantucket
by the great Cyrus Peirce, and sent
To support my burgeoning school, we spoke
with a candor I had never known. She came
without a bible, bearing just a trunk
of philosophy and natural science.
"I fear I've not fulfilled my parents
hopes for me," she said. "A good marriage;
a house full of children . . ."
"Nor have I," I said, "though
less and less I care, and who
knows, anyway, what hopes
my poor dead mother may have held
for me; certainly not for the life she lived herself."
I needn't have said more.
She understood, and likely
felt the same herself, since she
too had lost a mother. She was smart,
smarter than anyone I knew,
and loved and named the dried grasses
and wildflowers I had overlooked. It astounds me
even now how another mind, acute
to the world, can show you known things
as newly known. She did this
casually, her soft voice, soft face,
lighting up at the sound of words
she had never spoken aloud, and certainly
never to so avid an audience.
How beautiful she is, I thought,
and pleasured in the thought that I

too had something to give:
teaching the new recruit about self-
reliance, who to trust and of whom
to be wary; she being credulous and less
wise to the world, but also naturally
kinder and more forgiving: "These men,
who claim to *this* or *that*,
will rob you blind," I said;
and she: "Start by thinking best
of everyone, and let them lose your trust
only after great effort to forgive."
Perhaps it was her indifference to God,
her freedom from all that was doctrinaire
and severe, that made her kind;
as a warm wind is kind without knowing why.
A love has grown between us, deep and true,
and it fills my life in ways
never imagined. When her cabin
burned to the ground from a lightning strike,
she moved her scant belongings into mine,
and here we live—with Paul, our growing boy,
awash in a new and inextinguishable power.

   Rosetta Marantz Cohen

6. Ballad

Hedged by a cleft of ragged Indian Paintbrush,
our little garden thrives near the back stairs;
in front, a whitewashed porch, with rocking chairs,
a red door flanked by Yucca and Brittlebush.

Inside, Hoptree limbs in a glass vase
rest on a hand-spun, hand-embroidered cloth.
Into the open window now a moth,
a coddling, settles near Mary on the chaise

then starts again, as if some voice had called
him back to the sill, into the open air.
He hovers in the morning brightness there,
then flies unfettered into the boundless world.

PART TWO

A Modern Life

Word Problems

The heat of father's flannelled knee
against my own obsesses me,

and how his calloused fingers look
pressing against the opened book.

"Listen," he says, and reads as one
might read aloud to a simpleton:

"A speeding train departs at eight;
figure the distance and the rate."

My father holds a secret key
that could unlock this mystery,

but through my own uncertain stealth
I must discover it myself.

"Figure it out," he says, and then,
"For heaven's sake, at least begin!"

Up on the mantel Grandma's face
looks down behind a wall of glass,

and mother turns, as in a dream,
the pages of a magazine.

I hear the cruel kitchen clock
contemptuously tick and tock.

"Help me." I try to make my voice
bend down before my father's face

already dark with reprimand:
"You never *try* to understand,"

he says, and then he reads again,
but louder now, "A speeding train ..."

A speeding train departs at eight,
departs at eight from the darkened gate

and the soldier lights his cigarette
and thinks of a woman he has met

in another town, and the hands of fate
that impose this distance, (which is great)

and this rate of loss (a terrible rate).
"Hurry," says father, "it's getting late ..."

But anything now that I might say
wouldn't solve the problem anyway.

　　　　　　　　　　　　　Rosetta Marantz Cohen

Grandma's Bedroom, Brooklyn

Two twin beds stand neatly side by side
like an Amish farmer and his bride.

Hair pins sit beside a silver globe
on a shelf of the opened chifforobe.

And on the nightstand, on a sterling tray,
A sterling hairbrush, burnishing to gray

holds a knot of gray and yellow hair,
Scented of talcum, rose and lavender.

Grandfather's black boots, polished every night,
seem to consume and not reflect the light,

as they sit, like dark boats on a polished shore,
filled with the shadows of the Great War.

Light-flecked dust hangs in the still air,
marking the distance between here and there.

The Famous Poet Visits

Pale as the floral print of the host's settee,
you sit, remote, a fragile drooping flower;
while at your feet the tweedy pageantry
of your idolators ignore you passionately,
or try to match your grimace, dour for dour.
Back in the early days when your first book
was called "ecstatic" by the TLS,
you'd liked this sort of thing:
Some poetess, sprawled like an odalisque in a fauteuil,
could spark inspired visions of undress.
Your mind was fecund then; how effortless
were metaphors for every kind of joy!

Now it is different. Everything's the same.
The piquancy is gone. You say, "I guess
with age we lose some pleasure in the game;"
or so it seems now when some poetess,
leaning closely into your better ear,
inquires after your wife by her first name.
You sip your Coke pretending not to hear,
until at last your son says, "Mom is fine,"
shrugging (but subtly) at you with disdain.

Soon you will plead "a fever," slip to the street,
leaning against this Telemachus, you
will think of the grasses smothered underfoot,
the tiny birds that peck at the sewer grate;
will wind with him past storefronts dimly lit,
"Like faces from which all the life is drained,"
then back to the borrowed flat of a renowned
colleague, where you'll drink his gin
till dawn, and write the same poem again.

     Rosetta Marantz Cohen

The Kiss

"Kiss me," I say to Liz; at almost two,
her lips are cool and pink and petal-new.
So nodding to a tongue she barely speaks,
she lays her little hands upon my cheeks,
and shows me with a kiss she understands
the vagaries of parental demands.

My little darling, will you still embrace
with so much tenderness your mother's face
when she's grown very old and full of need?
Already in your dark eyes I can read
some future daughter, dutiful, whose kiss
hardly betrays its own distractedness.

Repair

Nothing repairs so poorly as a toy.
No cracked doll returned from mending
ever resembles itself new,
first flung from the box
amid paper and tissue.

Shoes, too, rehabilitate
like former convicts, shiny in the extreme;
replaced soles, replaced lasts,
but still the fact of *use*
eludes the cobbler's art.

Or friendship, once rent,
never gets un-rent.
Despite passionate retractions,
the cruel word thickens in the wound
like a missed staple.

Mourning too is a kind of poor repair:
distractions and platitudes,
friends' voices, the rabbi's
elliptical drone
stitch and suture,
but under the banded gash
permanently lurks the diminishment.

Rosetta Marantz Cohen

Land Grant School

The speaker was talking about the novel, how today
ecocriticism relies on too narrow a canon,
when suddenly, as if seized by an idea, the man on
the stage in the large auditorium turned away

from his notes to ask the audience of students,
"How many here have ever milked a cow?"
to which the erstwhile silent uttered: "wow!"
collectively, and roused themselves; feeling a sense

that something known and wonderful was here;
that plowing through this barren exegesis,
one may unearth a nugget of mimesis—
the moo of meaning suddenly made clear.

200 hands go up, slicing the air like sickles:
"Raised it! Milked it! Watched it go to slaughter!"
"Huh!" said the speaker, taking a sip of water,
then turning back to an essay by Ashton Nichols.

Children and Facts

There is something poignant in their love of them,
the way they hold a cool fact up to the light
and run their little fingers over its surface.
For them the bleak winter of the Pilgrims
conflates to a dense and tangible fact,
like something freeze-dried,
tart with a porous potential;
and all the Olympian gods line up in a row
ready to yield their power; dates,
names, battles lost and won, all
swallowed in their pure form; swallowed whole,
and born again out of the head, like Athena.

How fast that talent ebbs in puberty!
The mind, grown thick with subtlety and desire,
gropes its way toward facts, and finds at the summit
little of pleasure—"What is the point of this?"
The question, never asked in childhood,
now blunts the fact's first force, and then,
under the weight of abstraction, blots it out.

Rosetta Marantz Cohen

My Millennial

What you call *home*—
cat-pungent and damp as a sponge, cluttered
with flyers for *freegan* lectures, hot yoga—
mocks home, mocks comfort and the myths of childhood.
Irony dents the den's Formica floor;
anxiety, the stolid certitudes of the six o'clock meal.

Here is your American Dream: tributaries of desire leading
into a great sea of justice, where you and your kind
are liberated from me and my kind, and the poor are less poor,
and the rich, ashamed of themselves, retreat into peaceful,
compulsive philanthropy. Beautiful dream,
where poetry sings from the rafters in multiple languages.

You take on the cast of your time, there's no opting out;
swimming in the molecules of the day, bound by the digital
human, slave-wage-interned tourniquet
of the present. Poor girl:
When your media class ends, call me
and I will tell you again the way it all works out.

Gossipy Villanelle

We never were quite sure which way he went
(though well we know it isn't our affair)
Still, when he married, we wondered what it meant.

In college towns like this no harm is meant.
We'll stick our prying noses anywhere
To figure out who came with whom (or went).

Last year we all were sure which way he went:
Where is that Bill S. with the blond hair?
Now that he's married, we wonder what *that* meant.

Clea goes both ways. Does she resent
The marriage, given their affair?
We wonder if she wonders why he went

And married (why buy when you can rent?)
Or if he must, why then not marry *her*
Now that he's figured out which way he went . . .
Still, when he married, we wondered what it meant.

     Rosetta Marantz Cohen

Gifts from Foreigners

A wooden cup. A doll whose linen dress
smells of the sun-baked marketplace
of Istanbul or Marrakech or Thrace.
A pillow, small and functionless.

Also: a string of beaded yellow clay
which like the polyester square
of printed fabric I will never wear,
but cannot bring myself to give away.

Their faces gone. Their voices, like the sea,
blend into breaking sounds that sound the same.
Only these odd and useless things remain,
like a moral scold or a homily.

Frequent Flyer

Where the good and bad sit randomly
like playing cards in a deck, suspended
over the green felt table of the Midwest,
truths rise up in unexpected ways.

Once, between a structural engineer
and the Bridgeport postmaster,
we discussed the importance of prayer;
once, with an ex-marine, the supreme value of friendship.

Men, one often finds, are kinder
in the air; their stained ties falling
between splayed knees as they reach down
to retrieve a protein bar or offer to share their USA Todays.

Someone who owns a guardrail company
once fixed my laptop over Schenectady;
and someone who designs board games
ranked for me the best eastern casinos.

Among clouds, the distilled
lives of the world emerge and coalesce;
their essences condensed to one potent dose;
each, a short poem, read once and remembered.

 Rosetta Marantz Cohen

There were six of us at dinner

There were six of us at dinner:
Partnered for life, three women and three men.
We were staid, civilized, three women
And three men, all of a certain age.
Having weathered the worst and best
Of life; we had, in a sense, arrived.

It was late. We had all of us arrived
At that comfortable place after dinner
When we suspected that this was the best
Our lives would ever be. Men
Spoke about their teams, their stocks; women
About clothes, the indignities of age.

One said, "I have finally reached the age
when I am invisible to men; arrived
at a place where I am, in a sense, post-woman."
There was silence then, among us women at dinner.
". . . And I'm glad of it," she said, "to be free of men's
Sexual assessment. In school, I was always the best

In my class, straight A's, Summa . . . but the best
Thing about me, I always knew, was my age
And my beauty. I knew my professors, all men,
Saw only this when I would arrive
At their office hours. Or over dinner,
Later, with male clients—my sexual power as a woman."

And then the second of us spoke, the second woman:
"I called it 'flattery' in those days," she said, "Putting the best
Face on what was harassment; dinners
That ended in groped kisses from men twice my age."

And then I told them about the teacher who arrived
At my door at night, drunk, saying "I'm a man;

What do you expect?" How I had felt man-
ipulated and ashamed, and had never told another woman,
even though I knew the same man arrived
at other doors asking the same question. Perhaps it was best,
we said, that we had kept these secrets. It was another age;
we still ended up here after all: well-heeled, happy, among friends
    at dinner.

We studied our husbands as they spoke: good men,
Certainly; middle-aged fathers of daughters; and wondered
If other women were right now speaking about them at dinner.

                                          Rosetta Marantz Cohen

www.ingramcontent.com/pod-product-compliance
Lightning Source LLC
Chambersburg PA
CBHW032001140726
47988CB00019B/3089